CONTENTS

THE START OF FARMING

People have been farming for thousands of years and, in the process, have continually changed the world. Farmers have adapted different types of landscape to grow their crops: they have cleared rainforests, drained swamps and cut banks into hills. They have learned how to use the sea to grow seaweed and farm fish and shellfish. Today one-third of the Earth's landscape is used for farming.

Hunter-gatherers

People have not always farmed the land. Twelve thousand years ago, before the end of the last Ice Age, people had no more impact on their surroundings than wild animals. They hunted animals and gathered fruit and plants, always moving on to find more.

This rock engraving of people with cattle was painted between 3500 and 1500BCE, suggesting that farming had begun by this time.

Farming begins

Around four thousand years later, many people had settled in one place and begun to farm. There are no written records of this time so no one knows exactly why this happened. It may have been triggered by the climate becoming warmer in about 10,000BCE. This made it easier to survive and so the population grew. Perhaps hunting and gathering could no longer feed everyone so people turned to farming.

People may have begun farming by gathering seeds of the best wild food plants and planting them near their homes. Controlling herds of wild animals, an important part of the diet, may also have begun at this time, starting a process called domestication.

Follow it through: farming begins → Ice Age ends → The population grows → Hunting and gathering does not provide enough food

EARTH'S CHANGING LANDSCAPE

The Effects of Farming

Andrea Claire Harte Smith

FRANKLIN WATTS
LONDON•SYDNEY

First published in 2003 by Franklin Watts
96 Leonard Street, London EC2A 4XD

Franklin Watts Australia
45-51 Huntley Street
Alexandria, NSW 2015

Series editor: Sarah Peutrill
Series designer: Simon Borrough
Art director: Jonathan Hair
Picture researcher: Juliet Duff
Series consultant: Steve Watts, FRGS, Principal
Lecturer in Geography Education at the University
of Sunderland

A CIP catalogue record for this book is available
from the British Library

ISBN 0 7496 5155 5

Printed in Malaysia

Picture credits:
Corbis Sygma: 33 Baldev. James Davis Travel
Photography: 17, 35. Digital Vision: 8, 18, 21, 23, 24
(bottom), 26, 29 (top). Ecoscene: 25 Nick Hawkes;
31; 37 Papilio/Jamie Harron. Eye Ubiquitous: 7 Mike
Southern; 12 Miles Cort; 16 Stuart Wilson; 22-23
Howard Brundrett; 41 David Cumming. Chris
Fairclough Photography: 9, 28. Holt Studios
International: 39, 42 Nigel Cattlin. Science Photo
Library: 10 (left), 13 Jim Gipe/Agstock; 10 (right) US
Department of the Interior; 15 (top), 30 Kaj
R.Svensson; 19 (bottom) Simon Fraser; 20, 24 (top)
David Nunuk; 27 Nigel Cattlin/Holt Studios
International; 32 US Bureau of Reclamation. Still
Pictures: 6 D.Escartin; 11 Paul Harrison; 14, 36, 40
Cyril Ruoso; 15 (bottom), 19 (top) Mark Edwards;
29 (bottom) Gil Moti; 34 Romano Cagnoni; 38 B &
C Alexander; 43 Robert Holmgren. Front Cover:
Eye Ubiquitous/Stuart Wilson.

Every attempt has been made to clear copyright.
Should there be any inadvertent omission, please
apply to the publisher for rectification.

Farming villages   The first farming villages appeared in the Middle East (the lands around the eastern Mediterranean) in around 8000BCE. Early farmers often chose land along the banks of a river, such as the River Nile, where the soil is very fertile. This is because rivers sweep fine particles of soil, called silt, along in the flowing water. When the river floods the surrounding land, it leaves a covering of silt behind. Silt replaces the goodness taken out of the soil by growing crops. This makes the flooded area, known as the flood plain, very fertile.

The banks of the River Nile are still used for farming today.

A limited supply   There was only so much flood plain to be cultivated in the Middle East. This may have driven people to search for other areas of fertile farmland, so the impact of farming on the landscape began to spread.

People start to farm   The population grows   More land is used for farming

CHANGING THE LANDSCAPE

Farming has changed the landscape for so long now that it is hard to imagine how the Earth must once have looked.

Forests Much of north America and Europe was once covered in an ancient forest. Some of this ancient forest remains – in Scandinavia, Russia and the parts of Canada and the USA that border the Pacific Ocean. The rest was cleared for farming, building, firewood and industry.

In some places, new forest has grown up in its place, but it is often different to the thick, ancient forest that it replaced. Much of it is controlled by humans, who farm the wood as a resource.

Tropical rainforest Large areas of ancient forest, called tropical rainforest, remain near the Equator. This is also now being cleared to make way for new farmland, as well as for mining and roads.

Rainforests, like this one in Borneo, are the last ancient forests on the planet.

Follow it through: land reclamation

Easily available land for farming is limited

Farmers have to find new ways of creating farmland

Changing coastlines

Farming has also led to dramatic changes in land along the coast. Centuries ago, farmers built mounds, called dykes, to separate the land from the sea. The water behind the dykes was pumped out to drain the land for farming. This method of taking land back from the sea is called reclamation.

Case study: reclaimed land in the Netherlands

In 100CE, farmers in the Netherlands needed to create further areas of fertile land for farming. They built dykes to separate land from the sea. It was vitally important that these dykes, which were wide enough to carry roads, were kept in good condition, otherwise the sea would come rushing in. Despite the difficulties, these farmers were so successful at pushing back the water that today more than a quarter of the country is beneath sea level. This reclaimed land, called polders, is kept dry by a complex system of dykes, pumps, windmills, canals and drainage channels.

Flevoland

In 1927 the Dutch embarked on their most ambitious project: a 30-kilometre dyke across the entrance to an area of farmland that had flooded. The area that had been covered by water was so big that the Dutch called it a sea – the Zuiderzee (South Sea). After the dyke had been built, they partly drained water from this lake creating a new area of land, Flevoland.

Windmills in the Netherlands are used to keep water out of polders – land reclaimed from the sea by dyking and drainage.

Forests are cleared and land is reclaimed

Farming has a dramatic impact on the landscape

IRRIGATION

While some farmers created new fields by clearing forest, others found ways of using land where plants did not grow easily because of a lack of rain.

Irrigating crops Farmers with fields next to rivers had water on hand to give to crops in times of low rainfall. As they started to farm new land further away from the river, farmers dug irrigation channels to carry the river water to the fields.

An aerial view of a centre-point irrigation system for maize in Colorado, USA. Each field contains a long metal arm with water sprinklers along it.

Harvesting rainwater Others found ways of catching rain that would otherwise go to waste. Farmers have set up systems to capture rain that falls on roofs and spare land and to direct it to ponds or containers for storage. They have reduced the problem of evaporation from ponds by planting trees around the edge to shelter the water from the sun. This is a common technique used on the plains of China.

An aerial view of the canal of the Central Arizona Project in the USA. The canals and tunnels can carry about 2,000 billion litres of water per year. Crop-farming in Arizona would not be possible without irrigation like this.

Follow it through: wells The supply of water for farmland is limited Farmers find ways to grow crops on drier land by digging wells to keep plants watered

Going underground

Farmers have also developed methods to tap into hidden water supplies. When it rains, water sinks into the earth. It seeps down until it hits a layer through which it cannot pass. It then collects in the soil and rock, filling the gaps like it would with a sponge. This is called groundwater.

To reach this precious layer of water, farmers have dug wells down to it. The first wells were only a few metres deep. But as more water is used and drained from the rock, deeper wells have been needed. Now some wells can reach depths of half a kilometre.

A farmer in Mali irrigates his crops, which are in bunds – small enclosures which conserve water.

Take it further

Find out how farmers near you water their crops.

◆ Do they take water from a river or a well, or do they just rely on the rain?
◆ What do they do for water during periods of drought?
◆ Compare their irrigation methods with those in a region with a different climate.

The groundwater level drops

Wells are dug deeper into the ground

Farmers in India using a bullock-drawn plough to cover seeds with soil.

If you flew over the country in a plane, you would see a shifting pattern of farming: animal-grazing would give way to fields of wheat or vegetables. These changes are to do with several factors: rainfall, temperature, the nature of the land – whether it is flat or hilly – and the soil. There are many types of soil and some are more suited to one type of farming than another.

Cultivating soil

The first soils to be cultivated had to be soils that were light and easy to dig because farmers had only their own strength and a few hand tools.

The invention of the plough in around 4000BCE allowed many farmers to turn heavy soil and clear away natural vegetation in order to plant crops. They could now use much more of the land for farmland.

All sorts of soil

Soils vary depending on the size of the fragments of rock that make them up. Sand is made up of quite large particles of rock. Silt particles are smaller, while the particles in clay are almost invisible. They stick together, making clay a heavy soil to work.

Rock fragments also contain varying amounts of minerals, which plants need for growth, and different amounts of organic material. Organic matter – made up of dead plants and animals – provides food for the plant and holds moisture in the soil. All of these factors dictate what sort of plants the farmer can grow.

Follow it through: changes to the soil

Crops use the nutrients in the soil

Soil becomes drained of its nutrients

Crop rotation

Crops are a bit like people. Some like a particular food more than others. So farmers vary the crop that they grow to stop the soil becoming drained of one particular type of plant food. This is called crop rotation.

Changing the soil

Farmers have developed ways to change the soil they farm. They add manure from animals to boost the organic content or fertilisers to add nutrients.

Take it further

Look at the soil near you.

◆ Is it heavy or light?
◆ Is it made up mostly of clay, sand, silt, organic material or some other material?
◆ Ask someone who grows plants how the soil affects what he or she grows.

A field of alfalfa, grown to enrich the soil. Alfalfa uses nitrogen from the air to make nitrates in the soil, which acts as a natural fertiliser.

Adding nitrogen

Legumes, a group of plants that includes clover and beans, add nitrogen-based nutrients to the soil. So farmers plant legumes, such as alfalfa, where the nutrients in the soil have been exhausted.

This practice, although usually very effective, does not work all the time. In Australia, it has contributed to soils becoming too acidic for many crops. Farmers have discovered that soils vary widely, and that they have to be treated with care.

Crops are rotated
Manure and/or fertilisers added
Legumes are planted

The soil is constantly being changed by farming

ANIMAL FARMING

Farm animals rely on people for food and shelter.

Even before the earliest days of farming, humans tried to control animals so that they could hunt them more easily. This eventually led to some species of animals changing over thousands of years to become the cattle, pigs, sheep and horses we know today. These animals have come to rely on humans, while humans benefit from their meat, wool or ability to pull a plough or cart. In turn, the use of land for animal farming has had a major impact on the landscape.

Becoming domesticated

Humans have controlled how species develop. They would allow animals whose characteristics they liked – for example, animals that were meaty – to breed so that this characteristic would be passed on to the next generation. Other animals would be killed or prevented from breeding. Over time, this caused species to change dramatically in their appearance and behaviour compared to their wild ancestors. This process is called domestication.

Follow it through: animal grazing ⟩⟩⟩ Farmers graze animals on pasture ⟩⟩⟩ Animals eat certain plants ⟩

Overgrazing The farming of animals presents problems as well as benefits, however, and their impact on the landscape can be just as dramatic as growing crops. If animals are kept grazing in one place for too long, they will eat all the plants until the soil is exposed. A heavy rain or wind can wipe the soil away and the field loses its fertility.

In Lesotho, a small country in southern Africa, uncontrolled grazing of cattle in the mountain areas has caused the loss of the region's grass cover and destroyed most trees and shrubs.

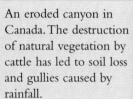
An eroded canyon in Canada. The destruction of natural vegetation by cattle has led to soil loss and gullies caused by rainfall.

Case study: sheep-grazing in the UK

Habitats have developed through centuries of interaction between livestock and landscape. The South Downs in England are low hills that would be covered with more trees and shrubs if it were not for sheep-farming. Sheep stop trees and shrubs from growing by eating the seedlings. This has allowed other plants to thrive, including many beautiful wildflowers.

Reverting back
Now that sheep-farming is in decline in this area, trees and bushes have grown back in some places, covering the grassy hills. To save the wildflowers, conservationists remove the bushes and trees, performing the role that was once carried out by sheep.

A farmer grazes her goats, sheep and cattle on endangered pasture in Burkina Faso, West Africa.

Animals moved to fresh pasture

Land is overgrazed

Field plants regrow

The soil is exposed and is eroded

Landscape is constantly changed

PROTECTING THE SOIL

Land that is farmed is often in danger of soil erosion. Every time soil gets swept away by wind or rain, farmers lose the land they work on. In the USA the average loss of soil per year is equivalent to the weight of a single-decker bus from an area of ground not much bigger than a football pitch!

Natural measures Trees prevent soil erosion. Above ground, they act as windbreaks. Below ground, the roots bind the soil together. Worldwide today, more trees are being felled than are being planted, and this loss accounts for about a third of all soil erosion.

Terracing land In mountainous countries farmers sometimes plant crops on terraces dug into the hillsides. This increases the amount of land available for growing crops and ensures that rainwater does not sweep the soil downhill.

Terraces are a series of steps and channels cut into a hill to divide its slope into relatively level areas. Each level reduces the amount of water run-off, so erosion is reduced. These terraces are in Indonesia.

Follow it through: soil conservation

Trees planted ▶ Roots hold soil together – trunks act as windbreaks

Leaves fall from the trees

Case study: the Dust Bowl, USA

In the USA in the 1930s, poor farming methods combined with a drought caused massive soil erosion across 390,000 square kilometres of the Great Plains.

Wind erosion

The land had been prairie (treeless grassland). High cereal prices encouraged farmers to plough up the prairie and plant wheat. This left the soil bare for part of the year. In other areas, cattle ranchers (cattle farmers) allowed their livestock to strip the land of plants.

From 1933–39 there was a severe drought. The exposed soil dried to dust and was swept away by winds on such a scale that the region became known as the Dust Bowl. Farmland literally blew away.

Re-educating farmers

In response, new farming methods were taught. Grass was re-planted along with 220 million trees that checked the wind and held the soil together. Today, people in the region know that the soil has to be carefully managed if they are to have a future in farming.

Take it further

Spread a couple of centimetres of soil on a large piece of cardboard. Prop it up at a gentle angle.

◆ Draw lines in the soil across the slope. These represent lines of crops in a field. With a watering can, lightly water the top of your 'field'. What happens?

◆ Now draw lines that go up and down the slope and water the field again. Which is the way to plant the crops if you want to keep the soil in the field?

Laid-bare Overgrazing (see pages 14–15) accounts for about a third of soil erosion. Poor crop-growing methods account for the remainder of soil erosion.

Good techniques to avoid soil erosion include planting crops in lines that run across the slopes of hills, and using spreading plants to protect the ground when it is not covered by crops. In some countries farmers build low walls of stone. These can catch soil and rainwater. Moisture also condenses on the cool stones, which benefits the thirsty plants.

In Niger's Keita Valley, a UN soil conservation project has transformed a barren landscape into a flourishing environment that can be seen from space as a green patch in the desert!

A farm in Lanzarote, in the Canary Islands, which uses low walls of stone to protect plants.

Soil is not blown or washed away

Leaves add organic matter

More moisture is kept in the soil

THE RAINFORESTS

The Amazon rainforest in South America stretches as far as the eye can see. It is hard to imagine a forest this big unless you have been there. Yet the clearing of the Amazon and other tropical rainforests in Asia and Africa has been one of the biggest causes of concern for conservationists in the past 50 years. Worldwide, rainforests have mainly been removed to make way for roads and crops and for the logging industry. It is estimated that an area of tropical rainforest the size of a football field is being destroyed every second.

Slash-and-burn Rainforests have been farmed for hundreds of years using a technique called slash-and-burn. Slash-and-burn involves felling one area of the rainforest and setting fire to the timbers. The ash adds nutrients to the soil. Crops are then planted, but the rainforest soil is poor and, after a couple of harvests, the farmers have to move on to a new patch of forest because the fertility of the soil has been lost.

The farmers can return to the land after about 20 years, by which time the soil has recovered and some of the forest has re-grown.

Burning Amazon rainforest.

Follow it through: farming in the rainforest → Road-builders or loggers open up new areas of forest → Farmers follow → They clear and burn nearby trees

18

Ruining the soil

The need for more land has driven some farmers to return to slash-and-burn plots before they have had time to recover. This can cause the soil to be ruined forever. Other activities, such as road-building or logging, have also allowed farmers to go further into the forests to create new farmland, meaning that the scale of the effect on the landscape is forever increasing.

A migrant in Sumatra, Indonesia, on land that was once rainforest. The trees have been cleared so that he can plant his crops. After a couple of harvests the soil will become exhausted.

Cattle-farming

As well as being cleared for crops, rainforest has also been cleared for cattle-farming. Ranching requires vast areas of pasture. In Central America in the 1960s and early 1970s ranchers cleared forest for their cattle. Today, ranchers in the Amazon and other rainforests usually take up land that has been abandoned by slash-and-burn farmers, rather than felling forest themselves.

Heavy loss

The loss of rainforest has several costs. It causes a dramatic change to the landscape that is the home of half the world's plant and animal species. It leaves the soil open to erosion. Finally, its greatest cost may be the effect on the world's climate (see page 21).

The forest next to this river in New Zealand has been cleared to create land for cattle-farming. The soil, which is no longer held together by the trees' roots, has slipped into the river.

They plant and harvest crops

Without trees, soil is washed away by rain. The soil becomes exhausted

Farmers move on

FARMING THE FORESTS

The forests that covered Europe and large parts of the USA thousands of years ago were removed to make way for farming, and later for homes and industry. Trees are also felled so their wood can be used for building, furniture, paper, cardboard and fuel. Today there may be a new role for tree-planting.

A Canadian managed-forest. This area would once have been covered in a variety of trees but has been replaced with a single species for efficient farming purposes.

This is an example of clear-cut forestry where all the trees in a whole area are cut down, rather than selecting only the largest. This allows rapid harvesting of trees, but it dramatically changes the landscape and affects wildlife and soil erosion.

An important resource We have come to appreciate the importance of trees to life on Earth, not just for the wood that is such a useful resource, but also for their role in the Earth's climate.

Follow it through: burning forests

Forests are burned to clear land for farming

Burning releases carbon dioxide

Less trees to take in carbon dioxide

More carbon dioxide in the atmosphere → Contributes to an increase in the global temperature

Trees and climate

By burning fuels such as coal, oil, natural gas and wood, humans have increased the amount of the gas carbon dioxide in the atmosphere. Scientists believe that this has caused the world's climate to change. We may be experiencing more storms, floods and droughts as a result.

Trees can reduce the amount of carbon dioxide in the atmosphere because they convert it into wood, locking it into the tree itself. Planting trees to reduce the carbon dioxide in the atmosphere may be a new use for forests.

But we are also losing natural forest. Some scientists are worried about the widespread felling in places like the Amazon. If we lose this means of locking in carbon dioxide, what will be the effect on global weather?

Forestry in the Philippines. Trees from tropical rainforests are some of the most valuable in the world because of the beauty and strength of their wood. A single log of the teak tree can sell for £13,000.

Reforestation

Five per cent of the world's forests are now plantations – forests planted by humans. But we are still losing woodland at three times the rate that it is being planted. Most people agree that more trees should be planted.

Case study: a forest in Mexico

San Juan Nuevo Parangaricutiro in Mexico is a town that depends on felling trees for its living. But the people of San Juan have chosen not simply to chop down trees and move on to fresh sites. They want to manage the forest so that it will be there for their children and grandchildren. They also want to make sure that the forest has plenty of wildlife – unlike some plantations that are more like factories. For this, and their good employment practices, their wood carries the logo of the Forestry Stewardship Council, the international symbol of good forestry.

INTENSIVE FARMING

The Second World War (1939–45) had a dramatic effect on the nature of farming. Food had been in short supply during the war. It is perhaps hard to imagine now, but eggs, butter and cheese were all a rare treat. After the war, politicians wanted farmers to provide plentiful, cheap produce so their countries would never have to go through such lean times again. This led to a major innovation: intensive farming.

Intensive farming uses huge fields and large machines in order to produce big harvests.

Follow it through: intensive farming

Politicians ask farmers to grow more food

Case study: UK hedgerows

The UK once had thousands of kilometres of hedgerows – put in place originally by farmers to create a boundary to their fields. They also acted as a windbreak and as a barrier to stop livestock from straying.

Bigger fields

The drive for more food transformed this landscape in the UK. Fields needed to be bigger so many hedgerows were replaced by fences, which take up less space and make it easier for large farm machines to manoeuvre. The loss of these hedgerows led to the loss of the wildlife that lived within them.

Fewer and bigger
Intensive farming means using more and bigger machines, bigger fields, less crop species, mechanised irrigation and artificial fertilisers and pesticides. For livestock farmers, it often means keeping animals indoors for long periods, using drugs to prevent diseases occurring, and, in some countries, giving animals drugs to make their meat less fatty or to produce more milk.

Animals on intensively-managed farms are often kept indoors and in cages.

Specialisation
Intensive farms tend to be specialised, growing just a couple of crops or only rearing chickens. The traditional landscape of fields covered with different crops began to be replaced with field upon field of the same crop.

In the 1960s, these techniques began to be transferred to developing countries to help them feed their growing populations. This was called the Green Revolution. Intensive farming techniques were enormously successful worldwide. Between the 1960s and the 1990s, farmers and scientists tripled the amount of food grown. It was a tremendous achievement. However, farmers soon found that there was a downside.

Farmers use bigger machines to help them to work faster
Fields get bigger
Farmers use artificial fertilisers and pesticides to feed soil and control pests

Farms become more specialised

MANURE AND FERTILISERS

A tractor spreading manure on a field. This is usually done before planting a new crop.

Intensive farming has led to cheap and more plentiful food, but some people believe that this has been at the cost of our rivers and coasts.

Using manure Before the era of intensive farming, farmers would spread the manure from livestock onto fields. This replaced nutrients taken by the crops from the soil and added organic matter.

With intensive farming, many farms began to specialise in either crops or livestock. This created two problems. The first was for livestock farmers – what should they do with their manure?

Too much manure? This has been a problem in the Chesapeake Bay area of the United States. Chicken-farming has become concentrated in this area; 6,000 chicken houses produce 600 million chickens a year and 750,000 tonnes of manure. This is more manure than the surrounding land can handle, so chicken farmers have to transport the manure to other areas. Some manure, however, gets into rivers and seeps through the soil into the groundwater.

Manure and chemicals put onto fields can get into water supplies.

Follow it through: eutrophication ▶ Manure and fertiliser are washed into rivers ▶ Water becomes laden with plant food ▶ Plant growth spurt (algal bloom)

Polluting water Manure is rich in nitrate and phosphate, which are vital plant nutrients, but they can cause problems if levels get too high. Excessive nitrate in water makes it unsafe to drink.

Furthermore, if these nutrients get into rivers they cause more plants than usual to grow. This is known as 'algal bloom'. When these plants die, they sink to the bottom and rot. Rotting sucks the oxygen from the water, killing the plants and animals that live within it. This is called eutrophication.

The use of fertilisers Farmers that specialise in growing crops have the opposite problem, but strangely it has the same result. Without any manure to put on their fields, farmers buy manufactured fertilisers. If they are not carefully applied, rain will wash them out of the soil and into rivers, causing the same sort of problems as manure.

In some parts of Europe, the use of fertilisers is now controlled to stop unhealthy levels building up in drinking water.

The surface of this river has turned bright green because of algal bloom. When these plants die, they will choke the life out of the river.

| The plants die and rot away | Oxygen in the water is used up | River wildlife dies |

PESTICIDES

Farmers face a constant battle protecting their crops against pests. Weeds compete with the crops for sunlight and for nutrients in the soil. Insects try to eat crops. Mould and fungi can damage a crop even when it has been harvested and is ready to be sold.

Pesticides Pests present a particular problem to intensive farming. Large-scale planting of one crop benefits the pests. To combat this problem many farmers have resorted to using pesticides – chemicals that kill the plants and animals that damage the crop. Without pesticides, intensive farming would probably not be possible.

A farmer in Japan sprays chemicals on his rice crop.

Follow it through: pest resistance

Pests eat farmers' crops

Farmers use chemical pesticides to kill them

Case study: the Irish potato famine

The story of the Irish potato famine shows the deadly damage that can be caused by pests. In 1845, a plant disease called *Phytophthora infestans* was brought accidentally from north America to Ireland. The disease infected potatoes, causing them to rot in the ground. In Ireland at that time, three million people lived on potatoes and very little else. The result was famine. A million people, one in nine of the population, starved.

The problem of specialisation

The effect of the potato blight would not have been so great if the Irish had not relied so heavily on one crop. They had been forced into that situation because of high land rents. Every other crop they grew had to be sold to pay the rent. It was a choice between food and their homes. Today, farmers in some poor countries are in a similar situation. They barely have enough food for themselves, but grow food for export in order to earn money.

Potato leaves damaged by the potato blight.

The downside Pesticides are usually sprayed on crops but studies have shown that they cannot be contained in one place. Rain may wash pesticides into rivers that are used for drinking water. Sometimes pesticides can be carried away from where they were originally applied. They may also remain on the crop, ending up in the food we eat. Some people worry that this could make us ill.

Another worry is that pesticides often kill creatures that help the farmer, such as insects that pollinate the crops or predators that feed on pest species.

Pest resistance! Pests can adapt if pesticides are used too much. This is worrying. Humans rely on just a handful of crops. If a pest of one of these key crops develops pesticide resistance, global harvests could be threatened.

Pests become resistant to pesticides

Farmers have to change the pesticide they use or find alternative methods to kill pests

Crop yields may fall

RUNNING OUT OF WATER

Between 1950 and 2001, the world's population doubled, and it keeps on growing. This means the supply of food has had to increase, and this requires more water. One tonne of wheat needs a thousand tonnes of water. The planet may be mostly covered by sea, but we do not have an endless amount of fresh, salt-free water that can be used by crops, livestock and humans.

The Murray-Darling basin is Australia's largest river system. It is a means of transport in rural areas, a source of water for farmers, a home for wildlife and a place of recreation for many Australians. It is vital to keep it flowing.

The loss of rivers With our growing need for more water, rivers are under pressure and are beginning to dry up. For example, the Murray-Darling basin is the heartland of Australian farming. The rivers that flow through it have suffered from algal blooms caused by high fertiliser levels, and also too much water has been removed for farming.

To keep the water flowing, the federal and state governments have agreed that no more than three-quarters of the rivers' water would be removed by people.

Groundwater Levels of groundwater around the world are also falling because we are using it faster than it is being replaced by natural processes. This is a serious concern. The water table under the North China Plain, which produces a quarter of China's grain harvest, is dropping by 1.5 metres a year. In Punjab in India, the rate is 50 centimetres a year.

Follow it through: water loss → Population grows → Crops, animals and people use a lot of water

Climate change The other problem is that the world's climate is changing. Most specialists in this area believe that this has been brought about by burning fuels, although the climate does change naturally too. Whatever the reason, the result is more frequent extreme weather around the world.

Droughts, certainly, are a big concern. But even freak storms may not help the water crisis. If a month's rain is delivered in a single storm, the ground becomes so soaked that no more can be absorbed. Rather than seeping through the soil to replace lost groundwater, the water floods into rivers and straight out to sea.

Running out By 2015, 40 per cent of the world's population will live in countries where water is in limited supply. In the Middle East, there has already been fighting over water.

Case story: the Aral Sea, Kazakhstan and Uzbekistan

The Aral Sea is a large inland sea in Asia. Water from the rivers that flow into it is used to grow cotton crops. So much water has been taken that the sea has shrunk. This has made the water in the sea more salty, causing fish to die.

Becoming a desert

As the sea shrinks, more of the sea bed becomes exposed. The soil dries up and the wind blows it away. The high salt content of the soil badly affects the plants that it lands on. These die off and the land turns to desert.

These ships are sitting abandoned on what was once the Aral Sea.

Rivers are drained
Groundwater falls

Seas and lakes can shrink

World water crisis
People conserve water

SALTING UP

Plants need special characteristics to grow in salty soils. Most plants struggle in salty conditions. Excess salt is a particular problem on irrigated land. It has been estimated that 400,000 square kilometres of irrigated land is affected globally.

Salinisation In Australia farmers lose some 2.5 million Australian dollars a year because of too much salt. In extreme cases, this problem – called salinisation – can even make the land unusable.

Crusting over Salinisation happens in two ways. If fields are given too much irrigation water, the water forms puddles, rather than sinking into the soil. The puddles evaporate, leaving a crust of salt on the crops and soil. The plants cannot tolerate the salt, and the crust of salt can sometimes be so thick that rain cannot reach the plant roots. The plants fail to grow and can even die.

Solutions include scraping the salt from the top of the soil, washing the soil to flush the salt away, adding chemicals, or planting crops that can tolerate higher amounts of salt.

A field in Canada that has been flooded by irrigation, causing it to be covered by a white crust. This crust is toxic to most plants, making the field unusable.

Follow it through: salinisation

Farmers clear land of natural vegetation

They plant crops which do not drink as much water as the natural vegetation

Rising water level   The second cause of salinisation is particularly common in Australia, which has very salty rocks beneath the surface of the soil. It happens after farmers have cleared away natural vegetation to plant crops. These crops may not drink as much water as the natural vegetation so, when it rains, more water seeps past their roots into the soil. This raises the level of the groundwater in the rocks beneath. The rising water table carries the salt to the surface.

Solutions   Planting trees may help with this. Their long roots take up lots of water and stop the water table from rising. Drainage channels can also be dug, but that then poses the question of what to do with the salty water collected.

A rising water table in Pakistan has caused this rice crop to fail because the soil has become too salty.

More rainwater seeps into the soil, the water level rises

More salt is brought to the surface

Plants are damaged or die

Farmers plant trees or dig drainage channels

DAMS AND FARMING

Dams provide one of the most dramatic examples of the way farming transforms the landscape. A river valley with villages and fields can quickly be transformed into a lake. The people and wildlife that live in the valley either have to leave or be drowned.

The versatility of dams

Dams are constructed across rivers to store and control vast quantities of water so that it can be used for irrigation, generating electric power, flood control, public water supplies, industrial water supplies and recreation.

Some dams serve only one or two of these purposes, but most modern dams have several functions.

The Grand Coulee Dam in Washington State, USA, was built to provide irrigation, flood control and serve as a hydro-electric power station. It is one of the world's largest dams and holds back a lake that is 240 kilometres long.

Follow it through: dams

Farmers upstream need more water

The government builds a dam

Dramatic effects

All dams raise the same issues. What happens to the people and wildlife that live on the land that is going to be flooded and what happens downstream?

A river may still flow, but it will be a fraction of its former size, disrupting fishing and farming. Farmers who live downstream – maybe even in a different country – will have less water for their crops and also lose the silt from the river that replaced nutrients lost from their soil.

The Sardar Sarovar Dam in India.

Case study: the Sardar Sarovar Dam, India

The Sardar Sarovar Dam was built to create a lake that would guarantee farmers in dry areas a year-round supply of water. To create the dam, the Narmada River had to be blocked and the homes of the villagers behind the dam were lost.

Protest

The villagers did not want to go. So they stood in protest as the waters of the Narmada, no longer able to flow downstream, backed up behind the dam and rose around them. Eventually, the villagers were removed by the authorities.

Benefits

The Indian government is convinced that the benefits of the Sardar Sarovar Dam outweigh the loss of the villagers' homes and livelihoods. The dam will not only provide water for farmers, it will also generate power as the energy of water falling from the top of the dam to the bottom is converted into electricity.

Farmers can irrigate their crops

The flow downstream decreases

Farmers downstream have less water and lose the silt that used to feed their fields

Conflict arises

GREENING THE DESERT

Dry conditions are a big problem for farmers. Without fresh water, farmers cannot grow crops or feed livestock. But with the help of dams and other methods, farmers are developing ways to change desert-like landscapes into fertile green fields.

Channels and pipes In Spiti, India, an ancient system of channels carries water from melting glaciers to desert farmers.

Libya has constructed the Great Man-made River, a series of enormous pipes that carry water from deep wells to farms. Others have built barriers across rivers to stem their flow – giving the water a chance to seep into the ground.

Converting salt water Some countries have invested in desalinisation plants. These remove the salt from sea water so it can be used for farming in regions with little water. This method, however, uses a lot of energy and is therefore costly.

A desert farm in the United Arab Emirates. In a desert climate, where there is plenty of sunshine, there are few crops that cannot grow – if water is made accessible, as achieved here through irrigation.

Follow it through: genetic modification

Supply of water is limited

Farmers turn to genetic modification

Intensive farming under plastic in Spain.

Take it further

Find out what your government's attitude to GM is.

◆ Are they promoting it, or against it?
◆ Why are people concerned about it?
◆ What do you think of GM?

Covered in plastic

If you see fields that look shiny in the sun, this may be because they are covered with plastic tunnels or sheeting that keep young plants warm and the moisture in.

Changing the crop

Farmers have transformed the landscape by bringing water to the desert. Now scientists are looking at the problem of a lack of water from a different angle: how to change crops so they can grow well with less water.

Plants can be cultivated traditionally by breeding one variety of a crop with another that has, for example, longer roots that can reach the water lower down. This is, however, a long process and farmers are looking to genetic modification (GM) to offer a shortcut.

Genetic modification

Every living thing has sets of instructions defining what it is like. These instructions are contained in its genes. Scientists can identify the genes that are responsible for a particular characteristic, such as 'suits dry conditions', and insert them into another living thing so that the new crop has the same characteristic. This technique could make a great difference to the landscape by enabling crops to be grown in dry areas.

GM also has other applications, such as creating crops that are suitable for salty soils or are resistant to weedkiller. Some scientists fear that the weedkiller-resistant crops could pass this ability on to weeds through cross-pollination. Thus they are concerned that this may lead to the creation of a breed of uncontrollable super-weeds.

Plants are created that need less water

The crops breed naturally with wild plants

Plants can survive in the desert

Wild plants spread to new a

More land can be used f

36

ORGANIC ALTERNATIVES

Follow it through:
organic farming

More consumers want
pesticide-free food

More farmers choose to
farm organically

G enetically
modified food
and intensive
farming offer ways
to meet the
challenge of an ever-
growing population
and a limited supply
of land and other
resources. However,
as we have seen,
people are also
concerned about
their effect on the
environment. This
has led some farmers
and consumers to
look for alternatives.

Organic farming In many ways, organic farming
is like old-fashioned farming. Some of the farms are
mixed, that is, they have crops and livestock. This means
that manure can be used rather than factory-made
fertilisers to replenish the soil. Livestock are grazed in
fields rather than spending most of their lives in a shed,
and they are not given drugs as a matter of course – only
when they are sick.
Organic farmers avoid using pesticides, relying instead
on 'friendly' insects to eat pests or planting smelly plants
near their crops to deter pests.

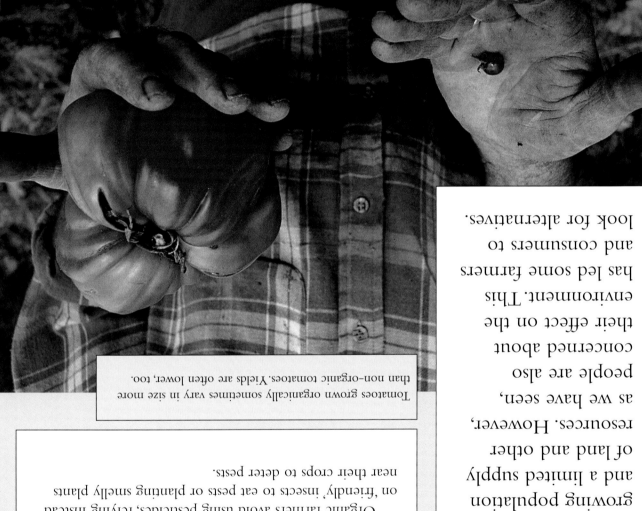

Tomatoes grown organically sometimes vary in size more
than non-organic tomatoes. Yields are often lower, too.

Studies have shown that the gatekeeper butterfly is more common on organic farms.

More variety

The other impact is that there is likely to be a wider variety of crops grown. For example, conventional farmers in the 'corn belt' of the USA may just grow two crops: maize and soya beans. Organic farmers would add in clover and maybe another crop too. This helps to keep the soil fertile without using manufactured fertilisers. In Germany and the UK, some water companies are even paying farmers to go organic because they believe it is cheaper than removing the pesticide that gets into the water supply.

Changing back?

Since very little land is farmed organically at the moment, the impact of organic farming on the landscape has yet to be established. However, more and more farmers are becoming organic, or partly organic, and this may mean that we will see certain changes.

For example, organic farmers tend to farm smaller fields surrounded by hedgerows and grassy banks for the 'friendly' insects to live in. If the fields are smaller, the insects can reach the centre of the crop to eat the pests. By encouraging insects, organic farmers also help the birds that feed on them. The Soil Association, which promotes organic farming, found that organic farms had 50 per cent more wildlife than conventional farms.

Take it further

Look on supermarket shelves to see if you can spot organic food.

◆ Does it carry a special logo?
◆ Does it cost more than conventional food?
◆ Does it say where the food comes from?

THE MIDDLE WAY

Planting hedges encourages 'friendly' insects.

Some farmers try to get the best of both worlds — a compromise between organic methods and intensive farming. They want the yields of intensive farming, which can be 40 per cent higher than organic farming in the case of cereals, but they also want to reduce their bills for fertilisers and pesticides.

Half-way house An option is Integrated Crop Management (ICM). This involves using clever ideas and technology to cut costs, while improving yields and helping wildlife.

Just enough ICM farmers use scientific equipment and computers to look in detail at the needs of each field. This helps the farmer to apply the fertiliser only where it is needed, rather than to the whole field as in conventional farming.

Reduces fertiliser run-off
More hedges and 'beetle banks'

Reduces algal bloom problem
Wildlife encouraged

Landscape changes

A 'beetle bank' next to a field.

Pest killers

ICM farmers try to encourage pest-killing wildlife in the same way as organic farmers. So they will keep the grassy slopes, known as beetle banks, in which 'friendly' insects can spend the winter. They will leave strips of grass and wildflowers around the edge of fields for the same reason. They might also plant hedges.

Luring pests away

On some ICM farms, farmers plant their main crop of oilseed rape (the plant that gives us cooking oil) with a variety of oilseed rape that flowers earlier. This earlier flowering attracts pests away from the main crop, protecting it from pest damage.

ICM farmers also try to use pesticide that will kill the pest and as few other insects as possible.

Helping birds

ICM farmers may also change their sowing times from winter to spring to help farmland birds. During the winter months, birds can shelter in the stubble left after the crop has been harvested. Stubble is also a source of food, but has to be ploughed into the soil before the new seeds are sown.

Good soil quality

Organic farmers need to plough to bury and kill weeds. ICM farmers, like conventional farmers, use weedkiller so they often do not have to plough their fields. They plant their seeds in small grooves in fields that are still covered by the remains of an earlier crop. This is good for the quality of the soil.

CHANGING EATING PATTERNS

What is your favourite food? Perhaps ice cream, chocolate, beefburgers or apples? Your answer to that question changes the landscape around you. If that seems far-fetched, then look at the facts.

Meat-lovers Between 1950 and 2000, the amount of meat eaten by each person in the world doubled. Most of this meat came from cattle reared on open grasslands. So people's love of steak and burgers led to open countryside, grazed by cows, and replacing forests.

Grain-eaters The meat of the future is unlikely to come mainly from animals grazed on grasslands. It is more likely to come from livestock and poultry that have been fattened up quickly on a supply of grain. That in turn puts great demands on the supply of grain, which is an important source of food, particularly for the world's poor. Farmers may have to find other ways to feed their animals, such as using crop left-overs, rather than valuable cereals.

Sweet tooth In the past 50 years, the world's population ate two and a half times more sugar and sweetener than before. This encouraged farmers to plant more sugar cane, sugar beet and corn, the main sources of sugar and sweeteners.

More of the grain grown in the USA is eaten by animals than by people.

Fish-lovers

Fish have been taken from the sea in large numbers over the past few decades. This has led to a fall in fish numbers. So farmers have turned to aquaculture — or fish-farming — to provide the fish that people want in their diets. Fish-farmers set up pens of fish, shrimps and shellfish just below the surface of the sea and harvest them like any other crop. People farm fish inland, too. They use large tanks or let the fish swim in fields of rice that are kept flooded with water. Fish are fed grain or pellets made from other fish. Fish-farming has increased four-fold in just 15 years and looks likely to grow further.

Getting richer

As people get wealthier, they tend to want to eat more expensive foods such as meat, fish, eggs, cheese and milk. The question is: where will all this food come from?

A fish-farm in Phang Nga Bay in Thailand. Sickness spreads quickly in fish farms and has spread to wild fish too.

THE FUTURE OF FARMING

Although changing eating habits have a huge impact on farming, the next big change that farming makes to the landscape will probably be due to climate change. The Earth's climate has altered naturally throughout its history, but it now appears to be changing because of the activities of humans. The climate is getting warmer, but the effects are more complicated than a couple of extra degrees on the thermometer.

Coping with change In parts of Europe, for example, summers are becoming hotter and drier – which is a problem for farmers trying to water their crops. Winters are becoming much wetter, which is also a problem – machines get bogged down on water-logged land.

How farmers cope with these changes will impact on the landscape. We could see countries change their traditional crops to ones they could not previously grow well, for example sunflowers and soya beans. Farmers could swap to varieties of crops that have longer roots and so can cope better with drier weather. This is where GM may come in, designing crops that can cope with less rain and more salt.

Sunflowers may replace traditional crops in areas that become hotter and drier as a result of climate change.

Follow it through: climate change

The weather changes due to climate change

An area becomes too hot or too dry to grow the usual crops

Pharming It might not be obvious to the average family out for a Sunday walk, but GM will turn fields into laboratories where GM plants are being grown for medicines, not food. This has been dubbed 'pharming'.

Forestry Forestry is likely to benefit from climate change. In the warmer climate and with more carbon dioxide in the air trees will grow faster.

Take it further
Find out what effect climate change is having on the weather where you live. Then look at the crops grown in your region.

◆ Do you think they will be able to grow well in the new conditions?
◆ What other crops might grow well in your region in future?

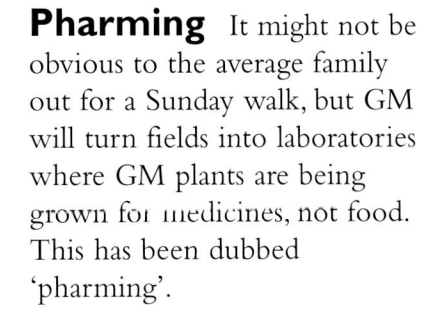

A scientist examines a genetically modified tomato plant.

A big influence
Farming will also have to change because it is one of the causes of global warming itself. Artificial fertilisers, livestock and the removal of trees all play a part in increasing greenhouse gases and therefore climate change. Once again farming is influencing the world around us – not just what we can see, but the water in the rock beneath our feet, and even the weather.

Farmers switch to other crops normally grown in hot places

The landscape changes

GLOSSARY

Agriculture Another word for farming.

Atmosphere The gases that surround the Earth.

Clay A type of soil made of very small particles. It can be very sticky when wet or very hard when dry. It is hard to dig.

Conservationist Someone who works to protect and retain wildlife and the environment.

Domestication The process by which humans have controlled certain animals and plants and used them for food, etc.

Eutrophication When too many nutrients enter rivers and seas and there is a spurt of plant growth. When the plants die they rot and suck oxygen from the water. This leads to wildlife in the water dying.

Evaporation Water heating and becoming a gas.

Fertile Soil that is fertile is full of the nutrients that plants need to grow.

Fertiliser Something that is added to the soil to make crops grow better. It can be natural i.e. manure. It can also be artificially manufactured.

Flood plain The area of flat land either side of a river that regularly floods. It is usually very fertile.

Genes The instructions held within each organism that describe its characteristics.

Genetic modification (GM) Giving a living organism some of the genes of another plant or animal so that it shows a characteristic of that living thing.

Groundwater Water that exists beneath the surface of the soil. It occupies small spaces between rock particles.

Integrated Crop Management (ICM) A method of farming that tries to reduce fertiliser and pesticide use on fields while boosting yields.

Irrigation System for watering plants using ditches or tubes that run along the ground.

Leaching Nutrients being washed out of the soil by water.

Livestock Farm animals.

Mineral A natural chemical within the soil. Some minerals are essential for growth.

Nutrient A food needed by plants and animals for growth. Minerals are a kind of nutrient.

Organic material/matter Usually refers to dead plants and animals, rotting within the soil.

Organic farming A way of farming that avoids the use of pesticides and artificial fertilisers and uses natural processes to boost fertility and combat pests.

Pesticide A chemical designed to protect a crop from either insects, weeds, rats and mice, or moulds.

Pollination	The transfer of pollen from one flower to another, enabling the plant to form its seeds.
Predator	An animal that hunts other animals.
Reclamation	Turning desert or marsh into farmland.
Salinisation	The process by which land becomes too salty for plants to thrive.
Sand	Particles of rock. Although they are still small, they are much larger than the particles in silt or clay.
Silt	A type of soil made up of particles in between the size of sand and clay particles.
Species	A particular type of animal or plant (e.g. there are two cattle species). Species of domesticated animals are further divided into breeds.
Stubble	The remains of a cereal crop after it has been harvested.
Water table	The point beneath the soil where the groundwater layer begins.

FURTHER INFORMATION

Forestry Stewardship Council
Manages an international labelling scheme that guarantees a wood product comes from a well-managed forest.

www.fscoax.org

UK Agriculture
A website to educate the public about farming. The site includes a history of the effect of farming on the UK landscape.

www.ukagriculture.com

Food and Agriculture Organisation
Part of the United Nations. Its aim is to help to make a world without hunger. It carries out research into farming and forestry.

www.fao.org

Australian Museum
Factsheets on farming and landscape.

www.amonline.net.au/factsheets/

Tropical Rainforest Coalition
A rainforest conservation organisation.

www.rainforest.org

Worldwatch Institute
A research organisation focusing on environmental sustainability.

www.worldwatch.org/topics/

Urban Programs Resource Network
A website with a section about the soil and how plants grow. It is designed for children.

www.urbanext.uiuc.edu/gpe/index.html

INDEX